Dženana Vucic is a Bosnian–Australian writer and editor based in Berlin. Her poems have been shortlisted for numerous prizes and her writing has been widely published, including in *Australian Book Review*, *Australian Poetry Journal*, *Cordite*, *Crikey*, *Kill Your Darlings*, *Meanjin*, *Overland*, *Sydney Review of Books* and elsewhere. Dženana is a fiction editor at *SAND* and the reviews editor at *Cordite Poetry Review*. *after war* is her debut collection.

Praise for *after war*

'Those of us who have never experienced war become distanced from such tragedy, willingly or not. Each poem in Dženana Vucic's remarkable collection, *after war*, asks us to look at, and not away, from destructive violence. There is beauty on these pages, as there is love, anger and loss.' **Tony Birch**

'*after war* exposes the devastation draped across a body, both one's own and the people around them. This white-hot collection challenges the disrecording of genocide through ferocious portraits that hang everywhere we look; in our homes, streets, skies and dreams.' **Hasib Hourani**

'*after war* is an unforgettable act of witness to the Bosnian genocide. This meticulously crafted collection strains against the seams of language and transcends its tragic contemporary relevance. Vucic's grasp on the endless echoes of manmade horror wrestles against her eye for the miracle of the soul's forbearance and the bewildering abundance of grace in this world. I inhaled this book and will be returning to it again and again.' **Jumaana Abdu**

'A formidable first book filled with terrible beauty, fury and power. Vucic's exquisite, unyielding verse shows us what it means to look closely at the horrors of war and genocide. This is a poetics of refusal: Vucic refuses erasure of her language, her identity, and her humanity. Vucic's is an astounding, important and original new voice in Australian poetry.' **Eileen Chong**

'*after war* is a stunning collection of viscerally unsettling poems charged by the cut, jangle and unbidden intrusions of the author's lived experience of the Bosnian War and its aftermath. It is, at once: memoir, trauma narrative, autoethnography, testimony, a history. In its wide-ranging interventions and interrogations, it is a historiography. In its apprehension of recent atrocities (Norway; Christchurch; Palestine), it is an indictment of the world's moral climate. In its resignation that 'there is only so much we can do with the violence of our past', it beseeches us to heed the present.'
Grace Yee

'Harrowing, compelling, highly sensitised and linguistically skilled, these remarkable poems take us on a journey through pain and bigotry, through love and familiarity, through loss and consequence. *after war* suggests we all have obligations to understand and care, to prevent such wrongs happening again and again.' **John Kinsella**

after war

Dženana Vucic

First published 2026 by University of Queensland Press
PO Box 6042, St Lucia, Queensland 4067 Australia

University of Queensland Press (UQP) acknowledges the Traditional Owners and their custodianship of the lands on which UQP operates. We pay our respects to their Ancestors and their descendants, who continue cultural and spiritual connections to Country. We recognise their valuable contributions to Australian and global society.

uqp.com.au
reception@uqp.com.au

Cover design by Jenna Lee
Author photograph by Leah Jing McIntosh
Typeset in 11.5/14 pt Adobe Garamond Pro by Post Pre-press Group, Brisbane
Printed in Australia by McPherson's Printing Group

University of Queensland Press is supported by the Queensland Government through Arts Queensland.

A catalogue record for this book is available from the National Library of Australia.

ISBN 978 0 7022 7112 0 (pbk)
ISBN 978 0 7022 7281 3 (epdf)

University of Queensland Press uses papers that are natural, renewable and recyclable products made from wood grown in well-managed forests and other controlled sources. The logging and manufacturing processes conform to the environmental regulations of the country of origin.

For Tomo Buzov
who stood up

after war

a memoir in poetry, in pieces

Contents

after, violence (cruelty, horror etc.)

ako bog da

there is no
chance
in the bosnian
family
only allah
only inshallah
only ako
bog da

ako bog da
there will be
no firing squad
but a car
with petrol
and no one
will notice
you slip away

inshallah
you will find
safety in a
stranger's house
and you will not
know what
it is he does
to you

allahu 'akbar
you will whisper
in the basement
when they come
for your mother
and she is
clench jaw
and follow

allahimanet
when your
mother takes
your hand
bears the weight
of your sister
across
a minefield

alhamdulillah
that you are not
another dead
girl another
raped girl
another body
in a mass
grave

there is no
god
in the aussie
family
only luck
only courage
only white
knuckles

still my mother
bends to her
prayer mat
tells me
thank god
and I say
thank god
for what

Between Aprils

after Gbenga Adesina

The first text message was sent as the year closed.
Before that, red-faced men stood and demanded

translation. They wanted us to know: *war is coming.*
When it started it was hours away, the troops sieging.

In the village we played with our dolls, our fathers
dealt cards and waited, our mothers looked askance

at the neighbours. A man told us that there was a limit
to community. He put a number to it: one hundred and fifty.

Dunbar's effect cut our village in two: Muslims on one
side, Catholics on the other. Back then people still shared

cigarettes made in their dead country, there were no
fences; we hadn't been told the news. The Pope forgave

Galileo in light of the truth. Elsewhere people died
in earthquakes, floods, mining accidents, school

shootings, plane crashes. People died in war. Soon
this would come to us, two armies rolling in to clash

across the street. Already a ghost had been seen haunting
the edge of our solar system while another stepped

daintily through a rainforest in Vietnam. We knew
nothing of this. We kept bees, raised sheep, picked

fruit. And when our army came for our neighbours,
we ran to the hills and hid.

First Year After War

When I am five or maybe six
and home is low-income high-rise,
margarine on sliced white bread and the clamour
of arguments no neighbours understand,
I watch from the lounge window
behind government-issue blinds:
this brand-new life
which is quiet despite the road beneath us, so quiet
Later we will cry at the machine-gun pop of fireworks,
drop to the ground, hands over head, when a car backfires,
flinch at raised voices
and unexpected bodies on the other side
of doors. Later we will make our own noise—
howl against the rattle of unmoored lungs
scream fists into pastsick bodies
throw ourselves awake drenched in shaking

But here is a moment of fracture, of still

I stare at the high-rise opposite, a woman
as she feigns at flight:
a moment of quiver and hold, of reach
the expansiveness of arms wide and encompassing
I imagine her to shout:
Gledaj šta imam! Ovaj veliki i bezgraniči život!
Look what I have! This great and boundless life!
And then she is landed, ungainled
I cannot hear her cry but surely—surely!—she must
I do not know how to uncouple noise from terror

Even in shell shock, there is the earbreak pitch
and all dying screams and whimpers and chokes

My mother says my name over and over
voice tilt with frustration
and I turn to her, sitting with a friend
on our government-issue couch
her friend who is *Australian*,
the first to sip coffee with her, eat *bickies* with her
even through the breaking
sentences and questions like *how to say* makaze?
(hand raised horizontal, two fingers extended)
Scissors I tell her and—
Neka žena je pala s prozora
But she does not hear or pretends
says to the Australian *scissors*
and there is laughter, delayed punchline,
politeness in the face of jokes that do not translate
I turn back to the window, the woman

How do you fall from a building unshaken by bombs
How do you fall unrunning from gunfire

At thirty, I will not remember
if I see the body or if it is a thing frankensteined
from shrapnel and exit wounds,
superimposed onto this idyllic suburban street
I will remember only that it is
five minutes before sirens

and the world becomes loud in the familiar:
shouting, a TV crew, men in uniforms, panic and rush
I will remember that I do not tell the psychiatrist
who earlier that day said
when the bad thing comes, you must not fight
turn to it and say: this is a dream and I am not afraid
But it isn't. But I am

Everyone knows not to stand near the windows

What is happened?
My mother is beside me, hand on shoulder
Her friend beside her, hand over mouth
A woman fell, I tell them and to my mother—
to sam ti rekla
Oh god oh god how awful
my mother and I are silent
It does not feel awful
Us, here, in this whole apartment
with our couch and our table
our unrationed coffee, milk,
a TV playing the news
and Sarajevo flashing bitter on the screen

Kvrguša in the New Millenium

We called it Bosnian pizza since we couldn't say its name. One of many things we couldn't get our mouths around. *Kvrguša, ljuljačka, cvijeće, četvrtak.* But also: squat. Antarctica. Squirrel. Sixth. Millenium. It was turning then, and my sister and I sat in the car practising its bends before the new year caught us by surprise. Mil-en-i-um. Mil-en-i-um. Mil-en-i-um. Mile-ni-um. Mile-nium. Tongues slippery over syllables, slipping. Our mother out there, quickly popping in.

Those days you cracked a window, left the kids in the car. Our windows stayed tight. When it got hot, we fought over them; my sister afraid of what might reach in, me afraid of what could not get out. Those days we were afraid of men, lived in a low-slung bungalow with saloon doors and bodies lurking unseen in the yard.

Once, my sister chased me around the house with the knife she kept under her pillow. The knife was for the men, but it had other uses. Once, my sister forgot to return it in the morning and our mother barrelled through the house in search, turned everything upside down until she found it gleaming in my sister's bed.

We had two knives. A little one and a bigger one. My sister took the big one. The one our mother used to break through chicken bone and slide through flesh, carving the cheap cuts before nestling each piece into a wide pan of dough. The one she washed, then used to cut the Bosnian pizza into thick wedges which we ate without plates, from the tepsija. A word we knew how to say. Straight from the oven was when it was best. Steaming, cream soaking into spongey pores. We ate with a fork and our hands, on the floor. Cross-legged in front of the heater, our mother seated furthest away. On one side, our arms burned with the grill's red heat; on the other, our skin prickled against the cold.

In the car, a man stopped to look at us. Leaned his back against the wall, hooked his thumbs into his belt. Grinned. My sister was always seeing men outside her window. The bad man, the bad men. In the car, her scream was an avalanche and it buried us until our mother came to dig us out. By then, the man was gone. The man was always going. On the way home my sister said mile-nium and I said, you're saying it wrong and my mother said, ostavi je na miru.

When I refused to eat meat our mother offered me the choicest pieces, digging them out of the Bosnian pizza with her knife. Gouging a hole. When I refused to eat meat our mother frowned and gestured, said, it's not meat, it's chicken. Gritted her teeth and said, eat. Gritted her teeth and said, please. This is how we learned to love. Gouging flesh, gripping knives. Calling things by other names.

it repeats / we repeat

my mother took up smoking after we escaped the war.
it didn't last long but the cigarette trembling in her hands,
the flick of the lighter—once, twice, flare—her face pale
against the summer, will outlast plastic & concrete & whole
civilizations. she was twenty-four once & I want to be dead
unfilled from her mouth & slid to the ground between
us & we buried it alive & we watched it spawn.

This is not the poem I intended to write, though it is the poem I am
always writing. I have said this before. I will say it again.
This is the poem I am always writing.

my mother is scrupulously clean, my sister too. we are a family
of compulsion & anti-bacterial spray. it is because we are
dirty. we have always been dirty. we bring the dirt with us,
between our skin & our hijabs, hoarded under the tiles of our
mosques, in the mouths of our imams & the meat of our halal
chickens. we bring the dirt with us until we are cleansed & we
have been cleansed & our country has been cleansed of us.

In 1992, *ethnic cleansing* took root & spawned;
undelimited, purposeless.[1]
Dissimulation is a purpose, though not a legal one.[2]

---

1 The term *ethnic cleansing* (etničko čišćenje) came to prominence during the Yugoslav Wars. It refers to the purging, by expulsion or murder, of an ethnic or religious group from a given area. It has no legal definition and is not recognised as a crime under international law.

2 Since the nineties, *ethnic cleansing* has been used in reference to the murder, detainment and expulsion of ethnic groups in, for example, East Timor, Sudan, Iraq, Sri Lanka, Syria, Myanmar, India, China, Tigray, Ukraine and Palestine.

my sister was born into a dead country, in need of ablution.
this is how we learned to be clean. it is more than taking off
your shoes when entering your home. it is learning: the home
is not yours. in the home that is not ours, 8000 brothers &
uncles are killed while their neighbours watch & we are raped
so that our children will not be like us, or worse: like them.
the home that is not ours is cleansed & we are cleansed.

I wanted to write a poem about language, but there is only the language
of looking away:
clashes
tensions
clearance operations
enhanced interrogation
collateral damage
conflict

Rubber bullets are just bullets with whitewash.

my sister was a little girl once; big wet eyes & a knife. spent hours
straightening fibres in her carpet so that each would lie just so &,
if disturbed, warn her: intruder. intruder. in case of dread: break
glass, remove hunger, chew. oh, but we have been hungry—little girls
with crusts of bread & sharpened stomachs. now my sister
is broken glass, jangling. the clack of her teeth begs & shards fall
to the ground & pierce our soles; & there are always little girls.

Years later people call it what it was: genocide, a word
that only occurs in past tense. It has definition, purpose.[3]
In the present, it would require us, if only to stop it.[4]

Other words that occur only in past tense:
colonialism
apartheid
concentration camp
slavery
torture

As such, we are not required.

---

3 Article II of the *Convention on the Prevention and Punishment of the Crime of Genocide* defines genocide as 'any of the following acts committed with intent to destroy, in whole or in part, a national, ethnical, racial or religious group, as such: a) killing members of the group; b) causing serious bodily or mental harm to members of the group; c) deliberately inflicting on the group conditions of life calculated to bring about its physical destruction in whole or in part; d) imposing measures intended to prevent births within the group; e) forcibly transferring children of the group to another group.'

4 Article I of the *Convention* provides that signatories undertake to prevent and punish genocide.

girl

I am watching her lick her blood off the floor and I am thinking: it is a marvel that the nose can lose so much and remain intact I am thinking: what is a fist a shoe a foot a book what is a belt a wooden spoon a frying pan if not a kind of missile. what is war if not everything that comes after it. I am watching her stand between me and pain and she is small but determined she is all raised chin and frown set mouth and grinding teeth and I am thinking: you cannot save anyone you cannot break suffering into even halves you cannot redirect a storm when you are living in it. I am watching her play at cheeky her tongue a brief waggle immediately regretted as the hand rises to meet it; I am watching the laughter fall out of her cheeks and her big big eyes shudder into expectation and I am thinking: where did you learn such lightness and why did you think it could live here, with us. I am watching her body slammed against walls until she learns to turn violence pre-emptive until her fists are bruises against her thighs until the scream has gone rancid in her throat until she is the wall. I am watching her waste away grow fragile and reedy then brittle and sharp; I am watching her transform into corners and I am thinking: can you shed the past like kilos or is trying to a kind of looking away. can you look away. I am looking at the wall and listening to her in the next room and I am thinking: the neighbours will hear this and part of me wants them to and part of me is afraid and I am thinking: please, be quiet. I am watching her slice off her excess which is flesh yes but joy too frivolity wonder the upward quirk of a mouth in full bloom and I am thinking it is a marvel that a girl can lose so much and remain I am thinking what is a girl but a body a fist a mouth big big eyes and all the yearning caught in her throat.

every day i cannot tell you

every morning my mother sends me a photo of the sun:
        its bruised rise over an ocean of slate
        tangerine mirror gleam across sand packed tight into low tide
        clouds leaking colour like fruit juice
                mulberry, plum, pomegranate, grape.
we have never been close
        we are getting closer. the irony of distance
        geographic, yes
                but not only.

every day brings us one day further from our history.
every day we find new ways to look east.

i have no anger left though
        there are days when you wish that i did
days when i leave your sky read but unanswered
        the sun bleeding itself through my pocket into my thigh, or
when you learn something about me from somewhere else
        and my silence becomes resounding.
there are days when you wonder what this means.
it means nothing.
it means only

in the west, you have bruised me the colour of sunrise;
        this is a thing you hold in your hands.
        i hold it too.
what i should tell you is that
        it is not heavy,
        that most days i do not feel its weight.

what i should tell you is that
    i am not a bad daughter because you are a bad mother.
you are not a bad mother.
    you have given me sunrise after sunrise,
    a sky so wide i have never felt its edges.
    you have built a world out of ashes, out of blood.

there is only so much we can do with the violence of our past.
you, too, have been the colour of sunrise.

eyes cracked open

A girl comforts her sister, small fingers clumsy on a dirty face.
Her sister's eyes crack open. She speaks in whispers.

I had a sister too, in the genocide. Not this one. Another.
When it was over, for a long time, we had edges,

brinks that jangled and grated. Now there are only shards.
Here there are only shards, scraps that jangle and grate.

When it is over, for a long time, we'll have edges—
not these edges, others. We too have sisters in the genocides.

They speak in whispers, their eyes cracked open.
They have small fingers and dusty faces, little comfort.

after, the wake; a keening

[Trigger warning]

and what I'm saying is sometimes you don't get a trigger warning before someone pulls the trigger, before you're a body in the wet heat pressed by bodies hunting insides. there are sixty thousand women in my country—at least—and I want more for them than our painful avoidance. yes! I want you to cry. I want you to feel the things you don't want to feel, which are anyway only a shadow of the things they did not want to. I know I'm being polemic. I know I'm being unfair. I know you don't deserve this but neither did they. there is so much unravelling which we are permitted to turn from and I've lost interest in your feel-good netflix binge, your escape from the escape that is your comfortable middle-class life. no one deserves this but some people must bear it and I want revenge for the sixty thousand women who did, the sixty thousand women who didn't get a trigger warning and what good would it have done them anyway. you don't get to opt out of genocidal rape. not if you're the victim and sometimes not if you're the man with the gun.

[Trigger warning: rape]
[Trigger warning: torture]
[Trigger warning: war]
[Trigger warning: genocide]

I'm not usually like this but yesterday a friend said *this is too much for me* and we have been friends for so long and her past has never been too much but mine, my people's, is an unbearable weight. another time friends could not watch a documentary about refugees and had to leave the room and me, there, the only refugee in the room, knowing the value of not looking away, of swallowing hurt that is not yours because it should not be theirs either and if this is the least we can do, we must do it. because sixty thousand women could have been saved and a hundred thousand people could still be alive if only we hadn't been watching *Law & Order*, if only we hadn't left the room. I said look at me when I'm talking to you! you won't believe the things I remember, the things I have seen and heard, the things that live rent free in my body and make my flesh a roiling parody of survivor's guilt. I have so much pain to milk—don't even get me started—but I'm not trying to force you to drink it, I just want you to know where it's from and how dare you deny us that?

I said look at us when we're talking to you.

Fainting Goat

My new housemate asks, do you scare easy?
Tells me I jump whenever I walk into a room and find
someone else already there
In the hall especially,
in the kitchen
Once in the living room I startle back
so quick I fall
socked feet scudding across the floorboards, cartoon-like
legs slipping out from under me
arse hitting the floor. Laughter
(this is not the first time I have fallen in fright)

He asks if there is anything he can do
which is a question I'm used to fielding,
being a person prone to public displays of terror
and internal combustion of the semi-private variety
I'm not good at holding things in
I'm all overflow and overwhelmed

What I want to tell him is: yes, change history
Please, change history. What I want to tell him
is my body has learned
to hold its fear, to cradle it
wound so tight it bursts out along
the seams of things:
a movement from one room to another
the crack between sleep and wake
a face between expressions and, especially,
any second of mis/recognition

The first time I hear a car backfire
I throw myself
to the ground,
arms over head as though arms
might make a difference
(they will not, they have not)

At new year's I'm taut like a last thread
watching explosions in the black sky
shop-bought fire crackers careening
down the street
like shells
I wait for impact
Really, I'd prefer to stay indoors,
windows shut to the moment
revelry curdles to panic

Don't get me started on a raised hand—
immediate recoil into my small self,
my vulnerable body
The stories I could tell you about hands
how easily they become fists
how easily they grasp weapons
how easily objects are
made weapon

What I say instead is: no. I'm sorry. Ignore me
I am the fainting goat of humans

What I mean is: if the worst is coming
I prefer not to know
(Walk home at night with headphones on, music blaring;
if I'm to be attacked I want to be surprised
I want it to be unexpected)
I do not want to run
and run
and still be caught

I have run, and run, and am still caught

triptych in which dreams are metaphors for survivor's guilt

i.

I dream my mother and I are carving
up the body of a boy—no we are draining
it with deep slices and pressure
squeezing out blood to make him smaller
to make him fit into history
I dream my mother and I are carving
up a boy and there are soldiers watching
our hands wet like organs and his blood
rises around our ankles, our knees
and his blood is an ocean thick with life
I dream my mother and I are carving
up a body but the body opens his eyes,
says he will show my grandmother what
I have done and meanwhile machine guns flint
in casual hands and we do not stop
I dream my mother and I are carving
up the body of a boy—no we are drowning
we are awash in blood and history
twenty-five years of silence and all
the things that cannot be buried, but must

ii.
it's the kind of restaurant we could never afford:
white tablecloths, crystal glasses, aperitifs
on silver platters, three different kinds of knife
& waiters in black wearing severe yugoslav faces
everyone eats steak, everywhere the high grate
of metal against fine bone china. every body
eats alone at tables set for two.

i am suspicious but say nothing. the steaks
are medium-rare, some blue. there are options
in terms of age, the marbling of fat, the precise cut.
our neighbours' white plates turn pink with blood
and grease; i go to the bathroom (i say).
in dreams you know when you are searched for.
i am searched for. i walk with care.

in dreams there are long hallways ringing
with footsteps; i walk down long hallways until
the footsteps are inside me and there is only
a door. a fridge. inside: carcasses strung across
the ceiling like lamb at a butcher shop.
suddenly, i am alone and i can take my time
choosing the right person to crawl into.

when the door opens i am closing her ribs, unafraid.
everything i have i owe to bodies like hers.

iii.
we are burning headscarves
we are shouting allahu akbar backwards
rabka uhalla rabka uhalla
we are filling crescent moons into dark suns
tossing stars into piles of southern cross tattoos
we are selling prayer mats by the stari most
calling them magic carpets, souvenirs
wrapping them in pages from the Kur'an
which we have dipped in nonsense
to void meaning
we are shouting sale sale everything must go
and praying for autumn to turn
all our greenness to gold

gone now

shall i tell u abt the time i started counting
things started washing my hands over & over
& keeping lists [i still keep lists] it wasn't an
ocd thing, it was a control thing, a serotonin
thing. nothing that a banana or 2 & some
lexapro cldnt fix. what abt the time i started
fainting just falling right over & out. lost 20
kilos on boiled rice & steamed veg but looked
so good they called it low blood pressure:
add salt to the meal plan & carry on. or maybe
that hazy time in my early 20s when I cldnt
sleep & the 3rd day awake meant a total trip
like thinking i was a cat or the tram was a
submarine & people's thoughts were fish, like
thinking things were falling apart [which they
were] but it's fine bananas are good for sleep too
& then there's always sleep hygiene, failing that
mirtazapine. actually what abt when i wanted to
be dead but lacked the energy for suicide what
abt when i started drinking @10am & whole
bottles of whiskey slipped down my throat like
breakfast juice what abt when i picked holes in
my palms 1st one then the other & gave myself
scabs like stigmata what abt the prozac days no
i don't remember the prozac days [i remember:
do not mix with breakfast juice] look, there's a
lot of what abts. there's a lot of words in general.
words for things like ur shaking leg like tktktktktk
against the floorboards for things like eyes wide

in the pillow for things like that hair caught in
ur throat its years of accumulated phlegm there's
words for this kinda ugly, too many maybe. what
i mean is: people will call u anything if it gets u off
their couch. now i am off their couch. ta-da.
shall i tell u abt getting better? i'm sry, i don't
know abt getting better. i know that 1 day i cld
brush my teeth & the next day i cld do it again.
this was an achievement. this was gold-star,
pat-on-the-head progress. i make it sound quick.
[maybe it was but i doubt it] the upside of ur head
falling off is ur memory does too. the upside of
this side is a whole lot of blank space. it was years
but they're gone now.

krenuli su vuci

I want to write a poem that explains the algorithmic slides that turned Karadžiću, vodi Srbe svoje into Remove Kebab when even google translate knows the difference; but how do you explain Dat Face Soldier backdropped by our dying and frontpaged to 800-plus threads on r slash The underscore Donald? What line connects wolves to kebabs, and how did we get from Bihać to Baghdad to Christchurch? Twenty years is a long march, even walking to that boppy beat.

I want to write a poem that explains how one genocide begets another becomes another betrays another and all that changes is what we call it and what we call them and what we call us; but first I need to know: is there a difference between a turk and a turk and do all wolves carry guns? If I tell you that ustaše means fascist, does that change what side of this war you're on? Which way does your trumpet swing and will you die for your führer if it means dying with us?

I want to write a poem that explains what happened when the wolves came, how they had packed away their instruments and pulled out their guns, how hardness came to settle on all our faces; but Karadžić got there first and it turns out genocide is not just aspirational, it's inspirational. five books since the war started and you'd think someone would think again but convictions prove thin when there's money to be made and there's always someone to appeal to.

I want to write a poem that explains a hundred thousand deaths, one point five million unhomed, up to sixty thousand raped and 9 million youtube views; but what can we do with this kind of history, the kind that playlists manifestos and turns people into bad meat. it's one thing to be a man trapped in a war machine with nothing but an accordion and teeth to grit, another to be the war machine, digitised.

I want to write a poem but our history is all references that make no sense and how do we remember ourselves when our selves are turned sheep, rewritten by wolves.

Remarks of the Closing

distinguished victims of the Closing
history sparks a resounding impunity
for humanity. ad hoc atrocities mandate
our raison d'être, they point to:
universality

a body distilled can be overcome.
war crystallised into universal value
The new paradigm will outlast every one
we commemorate legacy, are proud,
and secure in perfect realisation.
body in place, the Residual Mechanism

Today the winter solstice served to
gather the new afternoon, the sun
comes to an end. it will set but remain
look. the spirit embodied.
rekindle and endure.

after, silence

The Srebrenica Component

Count

with the Overarching

in pursuit

of permanently removing

days

shared

eliminate the Muslims kill men and boys

remov e women, children, elderly

this objective

through these means

genocide ; persecution

; extermination ; murder,

and murder, a violation of customs of

separation and
removal and
harm

With regard to
humanity,
inhumane Finally, also under
the terror
of men

a border separating
east a foot in the valley
continuity between holding and
capturing

taking and holding

Srebrenica

would isolate

and

engulf

Directive

devise a secure the

articulate in issue on

provide that

defend with

exhaust the , inflict the

force the

offer the

if they refuse, destroy them

subordinate

" inflict

loss , break

"

devastate

Thereafter,

famine prevailed. Men walk in search , but return empty

January

fell the day

, aim at
then control
lost men

captur e
control encircle
anticipate
attack

residents fled
a pattern
of “ ,
, before ,
, and and ”

torching houses a default
urged burn

burn

Most fell
Those who had fled fled again

February
not allowed a handful
. leaders
offer justifications such as
roads and bridges , snow , existence

weapons , money to be paid

Srebrenica

night

bore signs having been subjected

saturated ; people in and , in

, and in and

huddled

no food

water , polluted offal, excrement, oil.

deplorable

morning

grown hostile , swarmed

needed to be satisfied

enclave

left to roadblocks
deaths and
wounding .

beginning of the final
unimpeded

unabated

time
killed Protests
Ultimately

March swollen

predict last days.

consider a n d

observe

tightened grip ,

Calls to

presence

to UN protect and provide

"safe area"

in the meantime

seiz e the

day, pass Resolution proclaim

demand
ask

co-operate

Accuse

a cease-fire into force

hours

permitted to hinder and

disagree

negotiat e safe
delineat e safe
Thereafter

hills overlook the
arrival
(Bravo)

a battalion of
light and no more

earlier provisions
Pursuant , no one inside allowed
to have

Subsequently,

forbidden to

be

safe area

suffic e

to ,

with

Directive

strictly confidential

"

create unbearable situation total insecurity no hope of survival or life " To accomplish these goals,

restrict , reduce limit

the Muslim population, mak e dependant on good will avoid condemnation

"brea[k] and destro[y] the Muslims
"

repeat

"

unbearable situation

total insecurity no hope

"

The n assert never

minimise significance

suggest merely " " .

contradictions lack of candour.

testimony contradicted by the

ground

"operation pursuant

to Directive "

further elaborated

, wantonly violat e

"inflict heaviest loss

”

unbearable situation total insecurity no hope

subject all

justified by citing
and asserting
weapons

Thereafter,
lack led via
compromise

every tillable ground

sown with the reduced

the

fallen below , the denied , the

diminished

. people

subsisted on

short supply

survived on could

followed the

garbage truck to salvage

dwindling

Following the Directive , the

even worse.

April a halt to allow the taking Accordingly,

witness deprivation observe

call "*unobtrusively* reduce Muslim population"

that month diminished and subsisted until

end,

situation relatively calm a military standpoint

" feel of an open air prison".

Meanwhile, lines

flare

reconnaissance and sabotage

Muslim s

Late in the fall

r e S i s t

flew in violation of

soldiers seen arriving new and complete .

May

tension

forces

escalate

fire

shell kill wound

observe

request surrender

threaten force

attack

attack

openly

casualties, death

Meanwhile, carrying
On in
the

west

aware of both sides
, though on l y
on e

lacked freedom

and .

defens e

June

, a preparatory

anticipation

for implementing the

concept outlined

split apart and

reduce

separate and reduce

create conditions for elimination

gather prisoners

Final preparations made

observe tanks trenches
rocket launchers artillery and mortars
Snipers target
civilians, women and children

July

heavy and continuous
scattered the
hour s
fire

fire all over

fire

fire

fire

while, the collapse

Late evening

refugees stream

By then, already numbers

Srebrenica

audible , signalling

insecurity panic

meantime,

expressed concern

requested

withdrawal Forces replied

" using weaponry, thereby necessitating action.

reiterated

safe

conversations

"The President

is satisfied with

disarming Muslims terrorist s

demilitarisation "

"full protection

ensured "

"

a reasonable solution."

Bravo

Srebrenica tense as mortar

observe

frighted people

pour , their
villages burn .

an ultimatum

permitted to leave
, if they left behind

Bravo
humanitarian organisations

appeal
help stop

Forces
replied check information on ground call back

check information
talk again

night, soldiers
held a meeting

After, remain s

after,   piecing

white gravestones stretch the eye

Nearby, men and boys hide crimes
by dispersing remains
the truth is subject to a chorus
denial starts with official rhetoric
No Serb would deny that Bosniaks
were killed here … but a genocide. no
there were victims on all sides
the systemic slaughter *unfortunately*
a fabricated myth

This is the new historical reality
The genocide an inspiration -
Christchurch and Breivik
Nobel prize for Handke and a number
of revisionist statements

people who survived have to live
watching soldiers in the supermarket
separate history textbooks
trying not to hurt feelings

My father sits in a room alone

after Victoria Chang

i.

A boy drowns in the lake. Another steps
on a landmine. Years before, a man cocks his gun.
My father sits in a room alone. The village is empty.
My father tells a joke. A man hangs himself.
The punchline is: he hangs himself from a willow.
To understand this you need to know something of
the relative weakness of the wood. Bone will break
it. My father knows. My father is a lumberjack.
Two knee surgeries. Patella, in pieces. A scar like
a bullet hole in his side. Thumb tip cut off, sewn
back on. This is just the beginning. He has another
joke about hanging. The man cannot swim.

ii.

I'm tired of bean stew, of cabbage. Peppers
in vinegar. When winter comes, it's in jars.
My father and I do not speak the same language.
I am learning. *Prije rata, poslije rata*. Before the war,
and after. Before the war I sat in this room. After,
we were gone. Loss is too short a word for it.
Too small. How many letters in twenty-five
years. Some of us are still gone. Some of us,
still. There are no pictures on the wall. Photos
in a pile next to the TV. Papers. Dust bunnies.
Ash. Last year the forests burned. There were
floods. I didn't bring a warm enough coat.

iii.
There's always something to clean. Bathtub
slick with motor oil. Dirt. Small rocks caught
in the drain. Every light switch and doorhandle
smeared. I buy a new vacuum, new chemicals.
Sweep crumbs out of corners. My father's phone
plays ocean sounds: *Shhhhhhhhhh* in the night.
My father holds scraps of metal between his feet,
wears sunglasses if he remembers. Welds jagged
edges. Makes shapes. He forgets the sunglasses.
Sparks. Eyes red, weepy. Weeping. His phone
on speaker, max volume: *Shhhhhhhhhh*. Says *sorry*
can you repeat the question. Sorry I don't understand.

iv.
Every night we watch TV. Watch the news.
Watch *Survivor*, Turkish soap operas, sitcoms,
talent shows. My father chain smokes. Fingers
black with oil. Grease. Ash. The punchline is:
He wasn't in the attic. He was in the cellar.
This is a joke about April Fool's. On Balkan
Survivor one host is silent the entire episode.
He only speaks on the Serb channel. There, our
host is silent. No one stops politics. Flies on fruit.
This year was a bad harvest. Everything comes
from the supermarket. Apples. A watermelon,
guillotined. Brazen peaches, wet and sloping.

v.

We keep beer in the dishwasher. Rakija. Juice.
Soda, flat after opening days before. Weeks.
Since I came back my father does not drink. Back,
not home. Not yet. A woman walks a cow down
the street. Long skirt. Headscarf in the peasant
way. Later, a cow lows in a barn behind our house.
It is not the same cow, I don't think. In the war
we had a cow and then our neighbours were
killed and we had two. In the war fifteen people
lived in our house. More passed through it.
We milked the cows. Grew potatoes. Planted mines.
There's one Croat in the village. He comes to hunt.

vi.

I'm sick of not knowing what to say. This isn't
a big house. There's nowhere to go. A wasp
flies in, is lost throwing itself against glass.
Thinks better of it. One day there's a rhinoceros
beetle big as an apricot. Two days in a row
I'm stung by bees. I'm allergic to wasps, not bees.
My father wants to walk through the long grass
and dead orchard to a bend in the river. Wants
to throw sticks for my dog to fetch. He is allergic
to grass. Comes home with red welts on his ankles,
his calves. Pinpricks of blood at the surface
waiting to flood out. At home, we look for salve.

Gaj's Latin Alphabet

this year i go home and
spend six months parsing
my tongue around

the palatal lateral approximant:

ljubavi ljuljaška proljeće nedjelja

the voiceless postalveolar fricative:

šećer kruške naša slušati

the *voiced* postalveolar fricative:

žut svjež težak može tužna

i learn the difference between

ć and č
kćerka sjećam se / jučer čarape

learn how to say my name
the digraph

dž

how it takes up just

[one square]

in a crossword puzzle
how it sits round in my jaw
fills my mouth, boxy and serious

džamija džezva fildžan narandža

how it is not

đ
as in dođi as in rođak as in rođen

but not yet
how to hear the difference

gore gore gore gore

our equivalent of the grammatical joke
buffalo buffalo buffalo and etcetera
is gore gore gore gore
which, to an english speaker,
looks appropriate for a country
best known for its well-televised genocide

i write genocide both because it is true
and to avoid the glib rhyme that
english would produce
in bosnian, *gore* and *rat* do not rhyme
though, arguably, they are related.
our *rat*, for example, was the *najgore* genocide
in european history post-holocaust.
this is what we are known for: gore. war.
there's also a famous bridge.

if an english speaker heard it
gore gore gore gore
the trilled rs and vocalised es
would render it non-sensical
like so many buffalos buffaloing about

even google translate will not help
up up up it says and asks:
translate from croatian?
up above it says and asks:
translate from serbian?
up up up it says again.

if an english speaker asked about it,
if they asked some person who spoke
this language split four ways,
they would find out it means
up there, the hills burn worse
and this, too, seems appropriate for a country
best known for guns and landmines
in the hillsides around sarajevo.
at 1425 days, it was the longest siege
of a capital city in modern history
and is, therefore, memorable.

for bosnians too *gore gore gore gore*
seems appropriate. it is *nešto besmisleno*
and bosnians love to laugh, and know too well
the meaning of meaningless

Lemma

My *maternji jezik* is split four ways and if I ever wanted to sound smart—and I always do—I'd say I speak Bosnian, Croatian, Montenegrin and Serbian, but the difference is thinner than dialect and who cares if you say *hljeb* or *kruh*, scallop or potato cake? Signifiers are shifty and we shouldn't trust words anyway. They do not mean what they say they mean. For example: apology; bound; cleave; fine. Literally, I can't even.

We are pluricentric only in name, our mutual intelligibility higher than in standard forms of French, German, Spanish or English. But mutual intelligibility's a joke even if no one's laughing. I guess you could say *naš jezik* but it only makes sense if the *jezik* in question is yours to ours and if there's no other language to which it could apply. Another option is to call it Illyric, which avoids this kind of drama and makes us sound ancient and profound. Besides, it's true in some sense, but was more so before a certain Grimm Bruder got himself involved in *naš* business—and he was just the first. The world is full of men with too much time on their hands, drawing distinctions.

They say that Bosnian uses a Ijekavian reflex which is ironic since the palatal lateral approximant is an impossible sound. Or rather, it is for me. What I'm trying to say is: I want for us to be a canonical form, or at the least a coherent lexeme. There are advantages to meaningful indexation, you know. Clarity, for one. But also: easy translation. You see, I make it my job to be understood, which is to say: I speak other languages minimally and with a bad accent. Even my *maternji jezik* is riddled with poor spelling and mistakes of grammatical gender.

What more do I need than neuter and what am I supposed to do
with seven cases when everything I have can fit into one?
                                                                                    In English
there's no difference between being spoken to and being
spoken about and you'd think the vocative might clear things up
but every suffix is a vowel with novel stress and what is
an instrumental anyway except more noise? I'm sick of all forms
of conjugation. Aren't things complicated enough without us
always declining? I just want to be uninflected and least marked
but we're all suppletives with untidy roots and it just goes from bad
to worse, *loše na gore*. Maybe there's the rub: that nothing is infinit-
ive.

To Learn a M/other Tongue

I learn sustenance first:
trešnja, jabuka, mlijeko, hljeb
Learn to say nisam gladna before
I can say that I am, learn that I
must leave food uneaten since
empty plates are wont to be
filled with samo malo još

Then comes movement
(dolazimo, idemo, hajmo mi,
moja ćerka je došla)
and the whiplash of names
which sound familiar but are not
and which suggest directionality
or, at the very least, direction

In the stillness that follows
I learn to call things—ruka,
drvo, list, cvijet, nebo. My father
is a translator, he touches objects
and turns them to sound, stretches
his arms across naše selo
and renders the world legible

Speaking the self comes slow,
without intuition. I am not
cold, ali hladno je. To know
the difference I must know when
to uncouple myself and when to
double back. I do not miss you,
ali nedostajao si mi

Grammar proves stubborn,
forcing us into the perpetual
present. There's always someone
missing and we can never be
sure who did what to whom since
I conjugate poorly and without
regard to grammatical gender

In any case, we don't burden ourselves
with syntax. There's too much
history to get lost in semantics
and we're more interested in
the little things: gdje si, šta radiš,
jesi li gladna? Hajde, hoćeš ti kafu?
Drago mi je što si došla

Sevdah

noun

1. a feeling of combined pleasant, painful longing and contentment with one's life and the losses it has inflicted. See also, the traditional folk music of Bosnia and Herzegovina, *sevdalinka*.

I am full of black bile and this, I learn, is common to the people
I come from, who carry with them all the things they could not let go:
first love and second love
a glimpse of what could have been another in the easy smile
and working hands of a woman serving tikvenica
in Baščaršija
the whisper of red hair escaping her headscarf
the death of a sibling in infancy
the death of a child in infancy
the person you might have been were it not for Empire;
the people your children might have been
a Sunday in June and the gun shaking in Gavrilo Princip's
hands
our Comrade Tito and the promise of brotherhood and unity
the first trout you caught with your bare hands, but no one
was there to see it and your brother did not believe you
sitting in rahatluk with your neighbours Ennis and Mujo, Zoran,
Ivan, Marko, and Miroslav; with Bahra and Šefika, with
Ana, Gordana, Teodora, and Katarina
behara on the morning of April 6th, 1992
your brother, maybe his name is Emir or Ibrahim, a father
or uncle, cousin, their firm hand on your shoulder and last
words—*čuvaj se*

Srebrenica and 8372 of its men and boys
the house on Pionirska street, and the house in Bikavac, and all
the women and children inside them
etcetera
and etcetera

We are a people of black bile, of sevdah
from the Arabic *sawdā'*: black bile, melancholy;
via the Turkish *sevda*: love, strong desire, passion

Where I am from there is no love without loss and sevdah is
not words it is:
Albioni's 'Adagio in G Minor' for twenty-two days straight
a beauty contest held in a Sarajevo basement
fire falling through stained glass in the National Library
Aida's thin arms and the weight of the books in them
Admira holding Boško
wild strawberries in the fields where you are afraid to step and
blackberries bursting feral through cracked walls
homes painted aqua and tangerine, purple and pink and lime
green and why not
Bruce Lee cast in bronze, facing the apolitical north
stari most, rebuilt, still uncrossable, until you start walking
a minaret and a steeple, so close they could lean on each other
teens protesting in Jajce, refusing segregation
the words *moja ćerka je došla*
and etcetera
and etcetera
and exquisite, unyielding etcetera

Blagaj, Mostar

in memory of Fuad

The sky was crumbling; so full of sun it burned at the edges and hit the cracked earth of my aunt's garden in waves. It was a summer dense with figs splitting flesh on the tree. Pomegranates had burst open against the concrete drive, spilling their insides. On the steps: red chillis drying in neat rows on a white keranje she had made herself. Bundles of herbs. Thyme for čaj and sage to cure a sore throat. A tidy line of orthopaedic shoes, his and hers, a pair on each step. Months before the lilac had been in bloom, the forsythia. We had walked around the garden breathing them in, my aunt pointing to her silver beet, trellised beans, zucchini ripening against the soil. Neat rows of carrot and potato. The apple and cherry trees had just shrugged off their blossoms; there had been elderflower juice.

Today my aunt has cooked with a bountiful harvest: spirals of cheese and spinach rolled in pastry so thin you can see the new moon through it; quarter chunks of tomato and cucumber dressed in oil; spring onions in yoghurt; a loaf of fresh yellow bread. There's a watermelon cooling in the river for dessert. Beside it, too: plums, persimmons, ripe fruit scattered across the ground to be fetched after the meal. Inside: baked apples stuffed with walnuts and fried dough soaked in sugar. We are waiting for my uncle, gone fishing. If he's lucky, my aunt will fry a river trout or two—lightly, with a little flour, a little salt. Skin on and crispy. My uncle will make his same jokes, needling my kind aunt with her plum-soft heart. *Take this one away with you,* he'll tell me. *She's no good—just look at all this food she hasn't made.*

In the war, almost my lifetime ago, my aunt took her children in her arms and crossed the barebone mountains to our house. Hers had become a waiting grave. My uncle arrived every three weeks, a two-day hike each direction. Limping, he wore a trail into the stone earth to find her, to sit in her weather for three days. *Alhamdulillah* my aunt said. *Well, where've you been?* my uncle replied. Then he was gone. Then, as now, my aunt filled our plates: palačinke and uštipci when there was flour; pickled cabbage; stewed pears; bean soup stretched for weeks. My mother was a nurse in the village and in the evening the sisters sat together, drinking coffee when there was some, cracking walnuts between their palms, waiting for the men to come home. *Take this one with you*, my uncle jokes. But he would follow. He knows the way.

Above us the old fort looms its jagged teeth across the mountain. After coffee we will walk to its base picking blackberries and water mint along the path, then stand on the karstic lip overlooking history: a tekija where old Sufi clerics chanted Dhikr and where the mountain splits itself open to send our green Buna swirling past the house. They say that after his death, a great cleric had his body buried in seven tombs across the Balkans—choosing always small towns, out of the way places, so that as pilgrims made their journeys to honour him, they would spread the word that there are as many paths to God as there are breaths in a human body. My aunt knows all the names of Allah, though like all our people she says *sabur*, forbearance, most. My uncle is not a religious man, though he has been a pilgrim.

morning with window open

a door opens; steady stream of liquid; flush; thick cloth against thick cloth as the boilersuit is pulled over last night's clothes; clink of keys; front door closing; steps on the stairs; door opening; door closing; truck's engine stutters into a gravelly roar; five minutes, seven, of warming up; my father smokes a cigarette in the cabin but I do not hear it; crunch of tires in slow reverse, reassuringly heavy, slow; nervous sheep snicker, maybe they're goats; a woman walking down the far side of the street calls to a neighbour, gdje si; the neighbour calls back, pa evo me; *where are you? here I am*; a cow lows; a car whooshes up the street from my uncle's village; another rumbles down from my mother's; the gentle slope between gives *up* and *down* direction; swallows in the rafters; the way they gurgle and chirp, ruffling feathers; Jasmina calls Miralem's name across the beehives; a dog barks; then another; there is the hawing zip of a jay and on the balcony something sets the wasps humming; the dog bounds into the house and slips across the parquet floors; cicadas play frattoir in the long grass; the sheep—yes, sheep—bicker further up the hill; a single gunshot ricochets from nearby and into the valley; my heart beats in my ears, waiting for a world to have gone still;   the dogs bark, one and then the other; Jasmina shells peas into a metal pot, one plink and then another; the neighbour's son whirs down the street on a bike two sizes too big; a rooster crows; the woman adjust her headscarf, puts a hand on her heart.

Human rustling

When I find a scorpion on the stairs my father blames my dog.
Says she brought it in with her fur and enthusiasm. It scuttles across
the floor and is gone, to be found later, unmoving, in the bath.

That summer there had been a rhinoceros beetle on the balcony,
a great Capricorn on the landing. Hornets in the clothesline.

Everything was abundant, except fruit. Winter had been warm,
the blossoms came early, then the frost. Now, flowers are few but still
the earth crawls with life.

At the lake you cannot hear yourself for the horseflies, the rose
chafers, the bees and wasps. Pale and dusty Balkan blues drink
salt water from our skin, keeled skimmers swerve by.

New frogs breaststroke through the reeds, tadpoles wriggle in mud.
There are fish too, which splash out of the water and back in
incomprehensible leaps.

We see a snake slither into the blue and bend its way across the
mirrored sky to a tree on the other bank, far from us and our
human rustling.

On the way home, we see another looping itself around stones at the
bottom of a creek and throw rocks to scare it so that we can cross.

We find out later that she was harmless.
That when death came, we brought it.

after,

Gropiusstadt (Berlin, outskirts)

after Jenny Xie

To the south and east: shallow dish of open meadow.
City limits abut. West: two dark towers and social housing,
thick dark yolk of the supermoon. A balcony on the crisp
edge of autumn. It's a slow moonrise between right angles,
paralleled lines. Dense haze. Peekaboo in the clouds.

I didn't know they buried war rubble in flat-topped mounds
around this city. Maybe it's better to say that they laid it
in piles upon the earth. C points and says, this one might
contain pieces of the wall; someone told her so. This is the most
unassuming history has ever been.

Years ago, I tried to move home but found only foreign
countries. Yesterday I rode from N's house in a storm
and arrived soaked and glittering. A low hum: *I'm here I'm here*
I'm here.

I'm here. There's soup: boiled parmesan rind, peas. A teacup
for a ladle. The moon falls into our bowls, belly full.

April;

Early blossoms fall
with the snap of a late frost settling.

The stove in my father's house is fed on wood
unburned in our last winter.

His truck leaks diesel;
the earth cracks itself before receiving water.

My dry skin, scratched,
jumps free and becomes dust—
a tiny star system,
floating.

Storm clouds gather
while we look at our phones in the dark.

unutra

in the aureole,
sve je malo ludo
things happen far away
but distance makes immunity
because we cannot know
and we must maintain six feet

when the shelves empty
nema šta da radi
so we watch women fight over
keeping clean hands,
ljudi kažu: molim te
but it is hard to trust

life is shimmer and wait
ali u redu je. u redu je
bombs fall in other countries
so long as we keep them there
—our enemies liče na nas—
between living and dying

we are told to stay indoors
imamo mi vremena za sve.
hoarding toilet paper,
protecting what we hold
imamo mi dovoljno
concepts like *we* like *us*
like *enough*

Salt Whelm

We step into shallow
weather to find a tide turning
north, searching for a pole-

star, though halogen burns too
Many things, incandescent,
can be luminous, blinding

us to a soft-bellied being
possible only in the crepe-
scular hum. Silence

does us no favours, fills time
with ghosts and questions:
What does the sea know

of what we have done
to each other, to our
selves?

Here we are at the beached
shore of a world, stranding
against its edges,

waiting for a swell, a wave
from the other side, a light-
house to signal deliverance

unto, from
the wrecks we have left
in our wake

cut grass

a woman says
we eat the sand, we have no food

but we know that

in Gaza, the dogs eat well
in Sudan, vultures wolf the sun

after this is over
we will walk into the sea
in shame

when the lawn is mowed,
children eat grass

they have done this before

in Sarajevo, when the starving started,
people let go their dogs

poodles and great Danes
amidst sniper fire
watching families swallow weeds

in Srebrenica, in Murambi
in Kivu and Kharkiv
Kashmir and Rakhine

everywhere,

when a child is born
someone writes their name by hand

this is a knowledge we are made to forget

that hands turn to fists
that tender flesh

Weather

These days, evenings are heavy
with clouds that refuse to crack, to open
a window is let in the night
creatures, which flutter and tumble
into the glow of a phone

in my hand, where devastation lurks
behind every swipe. A flash
of lightning, then thunder peals
the breath from our bodies, declining
to touch. The wind

gales from the south and leaves
us stranded but not alone
in our thoughts—Weird how we can't stop
doom in our throats or make a sound
that isn't the opposite of rain.

Hamza

in memoriam

What's weird is that this morning
I woke up with your name in my teeth
I had a dream about you
or maybe it was about a cousin
on the Bugojno side
Someone I've never met
just seen
in photos
in front of the rebuilt city hall in Sarajevo
the rebuilt Turkish bridge in the town where I was born
Standing
young and earnest
in the face of our history.
Not unlike you,
Hamza hamza hamza hamza hamza
Until it becomes a purr in the deep belly
of a lion.
I hadn't thought about you in weeks
Not since you wrote
How bad it is!!
Trying to convince the world that you are dying.
That was months ago and
since then,
you have fallen silent and
since then,
have we been convinced?

There are rivers underneath the sea

Everything begins like this: with a shipwreck;
one body rent against another,
salt and silt,
waves lapping at the crest.
Howling.

What we aren't told is that there are rivers
underneath the sea;
that the world's largest waterfall
plunges
three
and
a
half
kilometres
through
the waters
between
Ísland and Kalaallit Nunaat
and that the Bosphorus flows both ways,
one atop
the other,
like a problem in math class:
a ball thrown west
on a train moving east, and so on.

There are many such mysteries
and we come to them slow, and suspicious

How, for example, can you tear
someone apart
without it floating between you,
an iceberg,

unmelting
or: what makes the undersea rivers flow,
avalanching
through valleys and canyons
into the abysmal plain,
then go still
for months, or years at a time
But return
or: where does all the water go?

Hadith Recorded by Anas Bin Malik

Even if	the	resurrection	were	established	upon
Supposing that		final hour	has been	begun	
Although		apocalypse	was	initiated	
Notwithstanding		Day of Reckoning	is	created	
Despite		catastrophe		decided	
When		Nakba		settled	
		end		founded	
		close		inaugurated	
				ordained	
				commanded	

one of you	while	he has	in his hands	a	sapling,	let him	plant	it
one of us		they have	in our hands		seedling,	let us	sow	
any of us		we have			life,		raise	
all of us					gift,		nurture	
					responsibility,		nourish	
							cultivate	
							sustain	
							tend	
							protect	
							home	

meantime

machines learn great thirst
rivers bare their hunger stones
in the meantime,
we burn a forest for the trees
make mountains from our plastic hauls
like things immensely

gently, gently
we manufacture consent
then deliver it from mines to factories
to houses neat within boundary streets

next day, express
click&collect
the future that was promised

some of us

wait for the turn

in the meantime,
ruderal plants rise
across the degraded earth
through shell craters and concrete
cracks in tarmac laid
over sacred ground

rise and turn their faces
to an unshattered sun

Because a wind blazes

through the soft hands of autumn
I let the hurricane burn
against my heart.
What else are we to do
with all this anger?
The world will end &
we will let it.

•

Every day a kiss is stolen
by one stranger
from another.
Every day a building
comes down
on a child.

They call this being
unalived.

•

This is the world that we are making:
Not everyone gets
to smell thyme on their fingers
or to cook a simple dish
for the one who holds
their heart.

Not everyone gets
a life in roses,
nor even in crumbs.

•

Yesterday I saw wild horses
graze a hillside, in the fog.
They could not look at me
nor me at them
for shame.

•

Men tell me that some of us
are worth avenging;
some of us are human
animals.

This is a logic
I've heard before,
having once stood
in a zoo & been fed
to lions.

•

The world grows small in rain
but does not stay that way.

•

Because after autumn there are
other autumns,
we learn to eat the wind.
This is what we shall do
with all our anger.

Eat the wind &
spit it out.

•

Sometimes the waves
will rise so high in our mouths
they'll flood out
& drown windfarms
off the coasts of rich
& modern countries.

Sometimes we'll open
our chests &,
teeth first,
throw ourselves
from great heights.

Do not mistake us.

This is the world &
we will take it.

•

This is the longest moment ever.
And this one.

And this

Notes

Cover

The image on the cover depicts the spomenik (*monument* or *memorial*) at the Makljen Pass. Variously named Pjesnik (*The Poet*) or Pesnica (*The Fist*), the monument was designed by Boško Kućanski to honour the Partisan soldiers who fought at the Battle for the Wounded (also known as the 'Battle of the Neretva') in which Yugoslav partisans defended the Neretva river valley and the Makljen Pass, preventing Axis troops from attacking the thousands of wounded Partisans in the hospital at Jablanica. The spomenik was completed in 1978 and destroyed by vandals using dynamite in 2000, leaving only the reinforced concrete skeleton. Neither the vandals' identities nor their motivations are known.

Dedication

Tomo Buzov was a Croatian retired army officer murdered during the Štrpci massacre. On 27 February 1993, Buzov was travelling on a train from Belgrade to Bar. As the train passed through eastern Bosnia, it was boarded by members of the Army of Republika Srpska who proceeded to check the passengers' IDs, singling out twenty ethnic Bosniaks, including a seventeen-year-old boy. Buzov, who was sharing a compartment with the boy, refused to allow him to be taken from the train and disembarked in his place. He and the Bosniak passengers were severely beaten, then shot, and their bodies thrown into the River Drina.

Some notes on the Bosnian War

The Bosnian War began in April 1992 after the Socialist Republic of Bosnia and Herzegovina passed a referendum to become independent of Yugoslavia, and ended not long after the Srebrenica genocide, with the signing of the Dayton Agreement in November 1995. It was fought between the three majority ethnic groups in Bosnia, the Bosniaks (Muslims), Croats (Catholics) and Serbs (Orthodox Christians) and resulted in the deaths of over 31,000 Bosniak, 2400 Croat and 4100 Serb civilians and 30,000 Bosniak, 5900 Croat and 20,000 Serb soldiers; as well as the displacement of over a million people and the rape of up to 60,000 Bosniak women.

This was a genocidal war, spearheaded by then-president of Republika Srpska, Radovan Karadžić, which aimed to 'ethnically cleanse' Bosnia of its Muslim population. It was characterised by indiscriminate bombings, torture and – as in the 1990–1994 Rwandan War – the use of rape as a weapon of genocide, primarily perpetrated by Serb forces.

The Siege of Sarajevo became famous as the longest siege of a capital city in modern history and the Srebrenica massacre as (so far) the only incident in Europe to be recognised as a genocide since the end of World War II. During the war, Bosniaks were under a military embargo and had little access to weaponry or defence, except that which could be smuggled across the Croatian border or which they won from enemy forces.

Bosnia and Herzegovina is now divided into two political entities, the Federation of Bosnia and Herzegovina and Republika Srpska, compounding ethnic divisions. In many places students attend segregated schools or segregated classes and learn different versions of history. Genocide denialism is an ongoing problem.

The name of the language spoken in the region is contentious. Speakers of different ethnicities tend to refer to it by the name that aligns with their ethnicity (Bosnian, Croatian, Montenegrin or Serbian). It is also known as Serbo-Croatian and more recently as Bosnian-Croatian-Montenegrin-Serbian or BCMS.

Between Aprils is written after Gbenga Adesina's poem 'The People's History of 1998' and refers to events that took place between April 1992 and April 1993. It includes references to Robin Dunbar's theory that humans can comfortably maintain 150 social relationships; Pope John Paul II's apology to Galileo and his lifting of the 1633 edict of Inquisition against him; as well as to the discoveries of 15760 Albion (the first object, after Pluto and Charon, to be discovered beyond Neptune), and the Saola (an incredibly rare bovid discovered by Vietnamese scientists).

It also refers to massacres committed on 16 April 1993, of which there were two. In the first, the Croatian Defence Council killed 120 Bosnian Muslim civilians in the town of Ahmići. In the second, the Army of the Republic of Bosnia and Herzegovina killed twenty-two Croats, including six prisoners of war and sixteen civilian villagers, in my familial village, Trusina.

krenuli su vuci references a propaganda song, 'Karadžiću, vodi Srbe svoje', produced during the Bosnian War. The song asks Radovan Karadžić to lead his fearless Serbs and warns the 'ustaše' and 'turci' to beware. The poem's title is taken from one of the lyrics and means 'the wolves are coming'. Turci is the BCMS word for Turks and is used as a slur for Bosniaks. Ustaše is a derogatory term for Croats and refers to Croatians who collaborated with the Nazis during World War II. Estimates suggest that around 500,000 Serbs were murdered during that war and 300,000 displaced. Bosniaks were not targeted because they were considered 'Muslim Croats' by the fascist regime. The Ustaše also operated the concentration and extermination camp at Jasenovac where – alongside approximately 16,000 Roma, 13,000 Jews, 4000 Croats and 1000 Bosniaks – around 47,000 Serbs were murdered.

The Australian white supremacist terrorist who shot and killed fifty-one attendees of a Christchurch mosque in 2019 played the song 'Karadžiću, vodi Srbe svoj' before his attack. This song, along with its accompanying video, had become a far-right meme under the name 'Remove Kebab'. The video features four Serb soldiers, one singing, one playing the keyboard, another the trumpet and the last the accordion. The accordionist has a hard, stiff expression and became known as 'Dat Face Soldier'. The video also shows emaciated Bosnian Muslim men in a Serb concentration camp. Prior to be taking down from YouTube, it had accrued 9 million views.

Karadžić is a war criminal found guilty of genocide, war crimes, crimes against humanity, persecution, extermination, deportation, forcible transfer and murder. He was a key figure in the Srebrenica massacre, which saw over 8000 men and boys slaughtered over three days. After the war, he went into hiding and was not arrested until 2008. In 2016 he was found guilty and given a forty-year sentence. In 2019 his appeal was denied, and his sentence increased to life.

He has published a number of books of poetry, including one directly before the war, two during, and three while in hiding.

Remarks of the Closing is an erasure poem of the Remarks by Judge Carmel Agius, President of the International Criminal Tribunal (ICTY) for the former Yugoslavia on the occasion of the ICTY's Closing Ceremony, as issued 21 December 2017: icty.org/x/file/Press/Statements%20and%20Speeches/President/171221-closing-ceremony-president-address.pdf.

The Srebrenica Component concerns the Srebrenica Massacre. In July 1995, the UN designated 'Safe Area' of Srebrenica was invaded by Bosnian Serb forces under the command of Ratko Mladić. Thousands of Bosniak (Bosnian Muslim) refugees fled to the UN compound in Potočari, hoping for protection from UN Dutchbat forces stationed there. Despite calls for assistance, the international community did not step in to stop the Serbs who, after capturing the city, unleashed a brutal campaign of rape, torture and murder resulting in the massacre of over 8300 Muslim men and boys while Dutchbat forces looked on.

Bodies were buried in mass graves, many of which were later dug up so that the bodies could be removed and reburied elsewhere. Efforts to find and identify the victims are ongoing.

This poem is an erasure of pages 2030 to 2076 of *Prosecutor v Radovan Karadžić*, the public Redacted Version of Judgement Issued on 24 March 2016, Volume IV of IV (not including footnotes). These pages describe events from May 1992 to 11 July 1995, leading up to the Serb capture of Srebrenica.

white gravestones stretch the eye is an erasure poem from 'Genocide denial gains ground 25 years after Srebrenica massacre' by Shaun Walker in *The Guardian*, 10 July 2020.

my father sits in a room alone is written after Victoria Chang's 'How Much' and takes inspiration from its first line 'A boy drowns in a lake. Another opens', reprinted with permission.

Sevdah references multiple aspects of Bosnian and Yugoslav history, including events of the Bosnian War and events since. Of these, most can be easily looked up. What may be less clear to readers unfamiliar with the region is that the names listed as 'sitting in rahatluk with' are traditionally associated with each of Bosnia's three main ethnic groups. *Rahatluk* comes from the Turkish *Rahat lokum* (Turkish delight). In Bosnian, it describes a state of peaceful enjoyment of simple pleasures – drinking coffee, smoking a cigarette, talking with friends. It signifies a relaxed atmosphere of contentment and security.

Mentioned, too, are two locations near Višegrad – the houses on Pionirska Street and in Bikavac – in which Serb forces trapped Bosniak women, children and elderly before burning them alive. Fifty-nine people were killed on 14 June 1992 in the Pionirska Street fire and sixty on 27 June 1992 in the Bikavac fire.

The poem also references, and hopes to honour, three people killed during the Siege of Sarajevo. Admira Ismić and Boško Brkić, 'the Romeo and Juliet of Sarajevo', were an inter-ethnic couple killed by sniper fire on 19 May 1993. Aida Buturović was a librarian in the National Library. She spent 25 August 1992 alongside her fellow librarians attempting to save books from the burning library and was killed on her way home.

The definition of *sevdah* included in the poem draws from definitions offered by Aleksandar Hemon in *Nowhere Man* (2002) and *My Parents: An Introduction/This Does Not Belong to You* (2019).

Blagaj, Mostar contains a reference to the ninety-ninth name of Allah: *As-Sabur* (the Patient, the Forbearing). In Bosnia, the word *sabur* (meaning patience or forbearance) is often said in difficult times, as encouragement to have strength.

Gropiusstadt (Berlin, outskirts) is written after Jenny Xie's 'Corfu', by way of Safia Elhillo's 'Amsterdam'.

April; takes inspiration from Robert Davis's 'Daily'.

Hamza contains words (italicised) that Hamza Ahmed (@Hamzahjazar) posted to his X account on 13 October 2023, amid the Israeli bombing of Gaza. He has not posted since. A man by the name Hamza Ahmed Mustafa Al-Jazzar is listed among the names of the dead of Gaza. He was twenty-four years old.

Hadith Recorded by Anas Bin Malik swirls out from three 2024 books that make reference to the hadith, namely: Larisa Jašarević's *Beekeeping in the End of Times*, Jumaana Abdu's *Translations* and Hasib Hourani's *rock flight*.

Because a wind blazes references Israeli Defence Minister Yoav Gallant's words when he referred to Palestinians as 'human animals'. The stanza following refers to Serbian propaganda spread in the lead up to the Bosnian War. Bosnian Muslims were accused of feeding Serb babies to lions in the Sarajevo Zoo. As with the false claims that Hamas beheaded forty babies, this disinformation was used as a justification for the genocide that followed.

The poem also adapts a few lines from Philip Schaefer's poem 'Suture'.

Bloody Moana contains a reference to the many catch-races [illegible] the Pacific; the [illegible] in [illegible] [illegible] when [illegible] [illegible] [illegible] [illegible] strength.

Crop-sand: [illegible] [illegible] [illegible] [illegible] Bloody [illegible]

Apologies is [illegible] from Robert [illegible] Dath.

Darab [illegible] [illegible] [illegible] [illegible] 2023 and the [illegible] building [illegible]. He has [illegible] since [illegible] is listed among the names of the dead of Gaza. He was [illegible] years old.

[illegible] Recorded by [illegible] [illegible] [illegible] [illegible] *Breakaway in the End of Time*; [illegible] [illegible] [illegible]

Because a wind blows [illegible] [illegible] [illegible] 'human animals'. [illegible] propaganda spread [illegible] [illegible] [illegible] [illegible] [illegible] As with [illegible] [illegible] as a justification for the genocide that followed.

[illegible] poem [illegible]

Acknowledgements

These poems were written between Trusina, Berlin and Naarm/Melbourne, where I lived and wrote on the unceded lands of the Wurundjeri people of the Kulin nation. The collection was finalised on Dharug and Gundungara Country. I pay my sincerest respects to these traditional custodians, as well as to the custodians of the other unceded lands I've called home: the Whadjuk Nyoongar, Turrbal, Yuggera, Kabi Kabi and Jinibara peoples.

This collection was born out of a project supported by the Peter Blazey Fellowship and the Marten Bequest, and completed with support from Red Room Poetry and Varuna Writers' House. I am grateful for the space – financial, physical, temporal – that these institutions allowed me to take for my work. I would also like to thank my fellows at Varuna, Kaitlen, Madison, Nam and Xiaole, for a beautiful time.

Versions of some of these poems have appeared in *Artist Profile*, *Australian Book Review*, *Australian Multilingual Writing Project*, *Australian Poetry Journal*, *Best of Australian Poetry* (2023, 2024 and 2025), *Cordite*, *Here&Now* (2022), *Overland*, *Peach Mag*, *Rabbit*, *Running Dog*, *Scum* and *The Crossing* (2023). Thank you to all the incredible editors who have supported my work.

In realising this collection, I am deeply grateful to the team at UQP. I would particularly like to thank my publisher, Aviva Tuffield, for her steadfast support over the years, and my editor, Felicity Plunkett, for her generous attention to these poems and all the thoughtful conversations around them. Thank you also to Lauren Mitchell for her sharp eyes and unfailing patience, and to Jenna Lee for this stunning cover.

Nothing of this could exist without my family, sprawling and complicated as it is. I am especially grateful to my sister, who is dauntless and striving and determined; my mum, who crossed mountains and taught us to be strong and independent; and my dad, who has been a harbour to each of us and who does not appear in this collection but without whom it could never have been written. Thank you, thank you, thank you.

Thank you also to my family in Bosnia – my father, my aunts and uncles and all my cousins: thank you for your love, patience and understanding. Most of all, thank you for waiting for me.

My writing and thinking are indebted to a world of incredible friends whose curiosity, wisdom, honesty and grace inspire me every day. Thank you to everyone whose conversations have left their fingerprints across my thinking and writing. There are too many of you to name but I'm grateful for every one of you. Insofar as this collection goes: thank you especially to Clea and Chiara for all your encouragement as I wrote this; Hassan for all the sprawling, twining conversations that led here; Kalid and Nigel for being my home away from home; and Morgan for being my biggest (and most indefatigable) cheerleader.

And thank you to Moritz, who holds all of me.